FOCUS ON MEDIA BIAS

BIAS IN REPORTING ON
POLITICS

by Connor Stratton

FOCUS
READERS.

VOYAGER

www.focusreaders.com

Focus Readers is distributed by North Star Editions:
sales@northstareditions.com | 888-417-0195

Produced for Focus Readers by Red Line Editorial.

Photographs ©: Michael Dwyer/AP Images, cover, 1; Shutterstock Images, 4–5, 7, 11, 14–15, 19, 20–21, 23, 25, 27 (map), 28–29, 31; North Wind Picture Archives/AP Images, 8–9; Chris Pizzello/AP Images, 13; David Guttenfelder/AP Images, 17; Red Line Editorial, 27 (pie chart), 39; Tom Williams/CQ Roll Call/AP Images, 33; Jeff Roberson/AP Images, 34–35; Ted S. Warren/AP Images, 37; Hani Mohammed/AP Images, 40–41; John Moore/AP Images, 43; Dang Van Phuoc/AP Images, 45

Library of Congress Cataloging-in-Publication Data
Names: Stratton, Connor, author.
Title: Bias in reporting on politics / by Connor Stratton.
Description: Lake Elmo, MN : Focus Readers, 2022. | Series: Focus on media bias | Includes index. |
    Audience: Grades 4-6
Identifiers: LCCN 2021008320 (print) | LCCN 2021008321 (ebook) | ISBN 9781644938638 (hardcover)
    | ISBN 9781644939093 (paperback) | ISBN 9781644939550 (ebook) | ISBN 9781644939956 (pdf)
Subjects: LCSH: Press and politics--United States--Juvenile literature. | Journalism--Objectivity--United
    States--Juvenile literature.
Classification: LCC PN4888.P6 S77 2022 (print) | LCC PN4888.P6 (ebook) | DDC 071.3--dc23
LC record available at https://lccn.loc.gov/2021008320
LC ebook record available at https://lccn.loc.gov/2021008321

Printed in the United States of America
Mankato, MN
082021

ABOUT THE AUTHOR

Connor Stratton writes and edits nonfiction children's books. He loves to read and think about how news media communicate about politics.

TABLE OF CONTENTS

CHAPTER 1

ATTACK ON THE CAPITOL

In the United States, **election fraud** is extremely rare. Even so, the issue worried many Americans in 2020. They thought it might affect that year's presidential election. Election experts did not share this concern. But election fraud received heavy attention from news media. President Donald Trump was a large reason why. In April 2020, Trump began speaking about it. He warned that election fraud would be a big problem. His

US news media produced many stories on President Trump's claims about election fraud.

statements led to major news stories. Some stories gave the impression that Trump's claims were correct.

The November election ran smoothly. No state found any widespread election fraud. News outlets reported that Democratic candidate Joe Biden had won. However, Trump did not accept the result. He falsely claimed the election had been stolen. This time, many news outlets responded differently. Some TV networks did not broadcast Trump's claims. And headlines often said clearly that Trump's claims were false.

Not all news outlets took this approach. Fox News, a conservative TV network, gave time to false claims of election fraud. So did several other conservative news outlets. Meanwhile, most Republicans did not trust the election results. In contrast, most Democrats did.

▲ Many of the people who broke into the US Capitol believed the 2020 election had been stolen from Trump.

On January 6, 2021, the distrust took a violent turn. That day, a mob of Trump supporters broke into the US Capitol. They tried to stop Biden from becoming president. The effort did not work. But five people lost their lives. The reasons for the attack were complex. However, the belief in election fraud was one cause. The attack showed how much impact media **bias** can have.

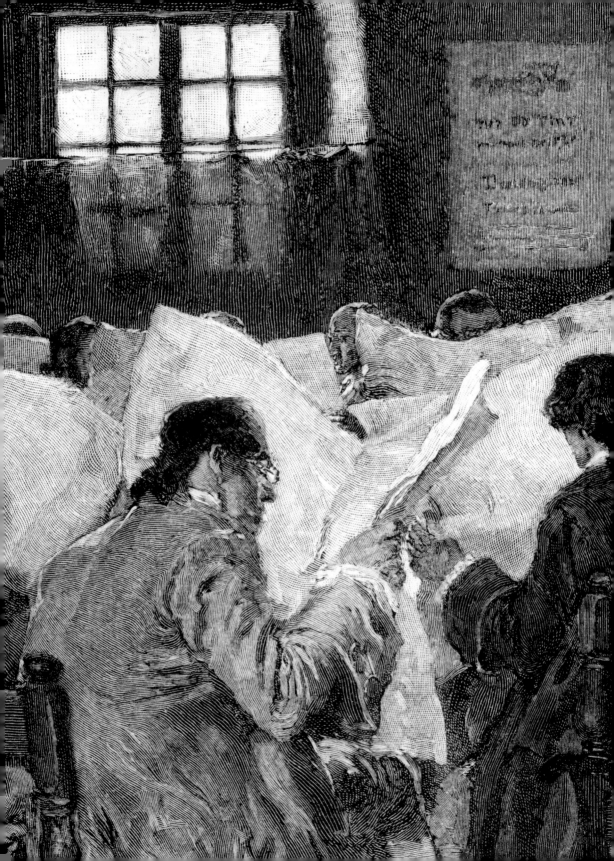

CHAPTER 2

HISTORY OF REPORTING ON US POLITICS

Politics has always been important to American news media. In the early 1700s, American news outlets largely reported on European politics. Papers in the American colonies changed focus in the 1760s. They began featuring articles that supported independence from Great Britain. These articles were not **objective**. Instead, they tried to convince readers to join the cause. In the 1830s, improved technology made it cheaper

In the 1760s and 1770s, some newspapers urged readers to support American independence.

to produce newspapers. Papers known as penny presses spread as a result. These presses reported more local news. But they sometimes made up facts to drive sales. Other kinds of political writing also became popular. For example, one paper featured strong attacks on slavery.

Conflict over slavery swelled in the years before the US Civil War (1861–1865). In response, interest in national politics grew. Dozens of newspapers started covering politics in Washington, DC. Newspapers played an even larger role during the Civil War. **Partisan** papers tried to increase public support for their side. To do so, papers often put out biased and false reports about the war.

Partisan newspapers became less common after the Civil War. One reason was that the news market changed. Large newspaper companies

▲ During the US Civil War, some newspapers supported President Abraham Lincoln, while others criticized him.

bought up local papers. These companies tried to appeal to wider audiences. Companies could make more money that way. So, they focused less on just one party's interests.

New technologies made nonpartisan reporting even more common in the United States. Radio spread across the country in the 1920s and 1930s. TV spread during the 1940s and 1950s. Radio and TV completely changed the US media landscape. People could access the same shows from all across the country. As a result, reporters were reaching much larger audiences. They wanted to attract listeners and viewers of both major parties. For this reason, reporters tried to avoid taking the side of either party.

This trend started reversing in the 1980s. Changes in technology again played a major role. Cable TV gave viewers access to several different news channels. Viewers could choose the ones they agreed with.

Online news took off during the 1990s. By the 2010s, Americans were getting more news online than from papers. And by 2020, online news had

> **THINK ABOUT IT**

What forms of media do you use to get news? Why do you use those forms and not others?

⟋ Cable news networks such as left-leaning MSNBC have contributed to an increase in partisan reporting.

surpassed TV. These changes had many complex effects. One change was a big rise in partisan news. Social media made this trend even more intense. People didn't just seek out news that confirmed their views. They also shared that partisan news with others. As a result, online news media increased feelings of conflict between people with different views.

CHAPTER 3

ACCURACY IN POLITICAL REPORTING

Politicians hold great power. Their statements can affect what many people believe. Their decisions can also cause huge changes. For these reasons, it's important for news media to report what politicians say. But politicians can make false claims. And by reporting those claims, news media may help spread that false information.

Reporters aim to be accurate. Fact-checking is one common method they use to achieve this.

One of the media's jobs is to inform people when political leaders make false or misleading claims.

Fact-checking can show whether politicians are being truthful. It can reveal false claims. In this way, news media can avoid spreading false information.

News media do not always succeed at this task. Reporting before the Iraq War (2003–2011) provides one example. The US government made numerous false claims to support its case for war. Many reporters, from both liberal and conservative news outlets, discussed these claims in their stories. However, they often presented the claims as facts. As a result, Americans tended to believe the claims were true.

Many politics experts argue that US media helped lead the country into war. The results of the Iraq War were catastrophic. Hundreds of thousands of Iraqis died. Millions had to flee their homes. Thousands of US soldiers died as well.

▲ The Iraq War resulted in massive death and destruction.

Accurate reporting involves more than just getting the facts straight. Reporters also work to provide **context** for those facts. If they do not, citizens may not understand the full story. Immigration reporting provides a helpful example. Researchers studied three major US magazines between 2000 and 2010. They looked at the magazines' use of images in their immigration stories. Approximately 75 percent of the images showed Latino people. However, less than half of US immigrants are Latino. In addition, more than 54 percent of the images showed immigrants who had entered the country illegally. But in reality, less than 25 percent of immigrants enter this way.

Researchers argued that these images created inaccurate context around immigration. In this way, the images told an incomplete and false story. These kinds of stories can have political effects. For instance, Donald Trump made immigration a key part of his 2016 presidential campaign. He often talked about immigrants as mainly Latino and criminal.

> ## ▷ THINK ABOUT IT

How can you tell if a news article has provided enough context?

During the 2010s, immigrants from Asia outnumbered immigrants from Latin America.

Reporters can provide context through a thoughtful use of images. They can also include more history. For example, immigrants often leave difficult or dangerous conditions in their home countries. And in many cases, US actions helped cause those conditions. With fuller context, people can be better informed about political topics such as immigration.

CHAPTER 4

SETTING THE AGENDA

Politics affects nearly all parts of people's lives. Governments make decisions about health care, the economy, the military, and much more. As a result, news media cannot give constant coverage to every issue that connects to politics. Instead, media outlets choose certain topics to focus on. These choices matter. They can affect which topics people view as important. The media's power in choosing topics is known as

Coverage of science news tends to be much lower than coverage of government and crime.

setting the agenda. An agenda is a set of issues that are treated as the most important.

News media tend to cover some topics more than others. For this reason, politics experts argue that the media's agenda creates biases. Reporting on **climate change** shows one example of this bias. Many scientists believe climate change is one of the most important issues facing humans. However, critics argue that the media does not cover the issue nearly enough.

As of 2021, politicians had not taken sufficient action to slow climate change. Some media experts believe this inaction is a direct result of low media coverage. News sources tend not to spend much time on climate change. So, many citizens don't think the issue is important. As a result, the politicians who represent them have not been motivated to act.

The media gives heavy coverage to severe weather events but often omits any links to climate change.

Political leaders often shape the media's agenda. Sometimes, leaders want to make changes related to certain issues. So, they try to get reporters to focus on those issues. That way, changes are more likely.

Many media experts claim that politicians set the agenda too often. Critics often point to Donald Trump's run for president in 2016. Trump regularly made **controversial** statements. These statements led to exciting news stories. And those stories helped media outlets earn more money. As a result, Trump received more media attention than any other candidate. That extra attention helped him win the election.

However, news media can play other roles in politics. Investigative reporting is one example. This kind of reporting digs up important information about a specific issue or politician. Investigative reporting can help keep citizens informed. It can even bring about changes in **policy**. In the 1970s, for example, reporters uncovered the crimes of President Richard Nixon. That reporting led to major changes in

> **THINK ABOUT IT**

News media, political leaders, and citizens can all set the agenda. Which groups do you think should have the most power to do so? Why?

▲ In 2013, journalists revealed that the US government had been secretly collecting huge amounts of data on citizens.

government **transparency**. It also helped change the role of money in politics.

People can set the agenda, too. Protests are one common method. People protest for many reasons. For instance, some protests are about gun rights. Others call for racial justice. Protests try to bring media attention to specific issues. That attention can put those issues on the agenda. Then, changes are more likely to happen.

LOCAL POLITICS, NATIONAL NEWS

National laws can be felt across a whole country. But local politics matter, too. Local media outlets can give citizens important news about the area where they live. Then voters can be better informed during local elections.

However, local news has been shrinking. Between 2004 and 2018, newspapers cut their staffs by nearly half. By 2020, more than 2,100 newspapers had closed. Meanwhile, large media companies bought up many smaller outlets. Big companies focus much less on local news. Local news may be available from online sources. But they face a number of struggles. For example, they often have a hard time earning money.

With fewer local reporters, people have less access to local news. As a result, national

7%
of US counties have
no local paper

44%
of US counties have
2 or more local papers

49%
of US counties have
1 local paper
(usually a weekly)

◤ Some people in the United States have very little access to local news.

politics sets the agenda more often. When that happens, citizens participate less in local politics. Citizens also become more partisan. For example, straight-ticket voting has surged. Straight-ticket voting is when a voter selects the same party for every race. Many politics experts worry about how these changes will affect US politics.

CHAPTER 5

COVERING THE HORSE RACE

News media tend to **frame** politics as a game. For example, campaign reporting often focuses on which candidate is more likely to win. This type of reporting is known as horse-race coverage. It has been common in the United States for decades. That's partly because US campaigns are long. They also involve many primary elections. Each election can be framed as one game in a series.

Politicians tend to receive less coverage for their views and more coverage for their poll numbers.

Large newspapers are more likely to have horse-race coverage. These papers tend to be driven by profit. Their leaders generally believe that horse-race coverage is more exciting than policy coverage.

Covering the horse race takes time. As a result, reporters spend less time on issues or policies. This trend was true for the 2016 US presidential campaign. News outlets covered candidates' policies only 10 percent of the time. Horse-race coverage also dominated the 2020 election.

Politics experts argue that horse-race coverage has negative effects. First, it can lower people's

> THINK ABOUT IT

Covering politics as a game can often be exciting. What are some interesting ways reporters could cover policy instead?

Horse-race coverage can make it hard for voters to learn which candidates share their views.

trust in politics. That's partly because it does not explain how candidates want to help people. Instead, reporters focus on winning and losing.

Second, horse-race coverage gives voters limited information. Often, they do not learn about candidates' ideas or plans. Without that information, voters may struggle to find candidates who best represent their interests. As a result, elected officials are less likely to reflect what citizens want.

GENDER BIAS IN POLITICS

In 2021, women held 27 percent of seats in the US Congress. It was the most in US history. Yet women made up 51 percent of the population. This lack of representation existed at all levels of government. Approximately 30 percent of elected state officials were women. And only 23 percent of city mayors were women.

Researchers have found that media bias likely plays a role. News outlets cover male and female politicians differently. Reporters spend more time discussing how the women look. In addition, reporters are more likely to describe women as too aggressive. Politics experts say these biases may explain why fewer women hold elected offices.

Republican representatives Young Kim and Michelle Steel entered the US Congress in 2021.

Media bias tends to be stronger against women of color. Researchers have begun studying this kind of bias in US politics. For example, researchers examined US elections in 2006 and 2012. In both years, white female candidates received more coverage than Black and Latina female candidates. Media attention helps voters learn about candidates. But if a candidate receives less media attention, she may struggle to get elected. Despite these barriers, a record number of women of color entered Congress in 2021.

CHAPTER 6

POLITICAL MEDIA

Researchers have looked for partisan bias in US media. As a whole, US media shows little bias in favor of one party or the other. However, many individual outlets lean toward one party. Some do so on purpose. These outlets do not claim to be unbiased. Instead, they highlight the views of the left or the right. Other outlets focus on specific points of view. For example, Black presses have a long history in the United States.

Sean Hannity of Fox News offers viewers a conservative perspective.

These papers focus on the experiences of Black people. The experiences of Black people tend to be underrepresented in major media outlets.

Major media outlets do cover some Black experiences. But this coverage may be shaped by bias. For instance, media experts studied how US news outlets cover protests. In 2017, some protests opposed President Trump. Others opposed police violence against Black people. Experts found that the two protests received different kinds of attention. Overall, anti-Trump protests received more positive coverage. Black Lives Matter protests received more negative attention. Media coverage can affect how people view the protests. In addition, it can impact how people view the issues raised by the protesters.

Some news sources try to avoid leaning toward one party. This approach faces different

Coverage of Black Lives Matter protests tended to be more negative than coverage of protests against President Trump.

challenges. One major challenge is known as false balance. False balance happens when the media presents unequal sides as if they are equal.

Many critics believe false balance happened during the 2016 presidential campaign. That year, Donald Trump ran against Hillary Clinton. Both Trump and Clinton were connected to scandals.

Clinton had used personal email for government work, which is against the law. In contrast, Trump faced accusations of sexual assault, fraud, racism, and more. Even so, reporters covered Clinton's email more than all of Trump's scandals put together. Reporters tried not to favor one party over the other. But critics argued that this was false balance. It made readers think the scandals were equally serious.

Reporting on politics has always been tricky. Online news and social media have increased this complexity. On the one hand, people can choose from more sources than ever before. That choice helps people find the information they want. On the other hand, media experts believe online media can increase political divides. People use social media to seek out news that confirms their beliefs. Online **algorithms** also play a role. They suggest new content that reflects users' beliefs. As a result, people of different parties often receive completely different information. When that happens, they can become less able to find common ground.

TRUSTING SOURCES ◄

The news sources that Americans trust depend on their political beliefs. Researchers have found that liberals and conservatives tend to trust different sources.

	Liberal	Left-leaning	Center	Right-leaning	Conservative
PBS	✓	✓	✓	O	✗
ABC	✓	✓	✓	✓	✗
CBS	✓	✓	✓	O	✗
NBC	✓	✓	✓	O	✗
CNN	✓	✓	✓	O	✗
Fox News	✗	✗	✓	✓	✓

✓ trust   O equal trust and distrust   ✗ distrust

CHAPTER 7

THE UNITED STATES AND THE WORLD

The United States holds enormous power in the world. As of 2021, it had the world's largest economy. It also had the world's strongest military. During the late 2010s, US forces were active in at least 80 countries around the globe. The US government also directly influences leaders and trade in dozens of countries.

However, US media spends little time on world events. Most Americans come across very

The war in Yemen has caused enormous devastation but has received very little coverage from US media sources.

little world news. As a result, they often don't know much about other countries. In contrast, US politics receives huge amounts of attention around the world.

When US media does cover world events, certain biases are common. One trend is that world news is framed in terms of US interests. Reporters focus less on the interests of the countries they are covering. Another trend involves war coverage. News media tend to avoid talking about deaths from wars. This can leave people unaware of the wars' true costs. And war is often devastating. It can lead to huge losses of life. It can destroy societies and governments.

Finally, world news often reflects the views of the US government. That's partly because reporters depend heavily on government officials for information. Officials from both major parties

⚓ During the Iraq War, American reporters tended to focus more on US soldiers than on Iraqi civilians.

tend to share many views about foreign policy. For the most part, they support the government's actions. Few offer disagreement or criticism. Because reporters use these officials as sources, news stories often reflect their views.

This last bias can be especially important. Citizens depend on news media to form opinions. If news media simply repeat government claims, citizens will struggle to make informed decisions about the government's actions.

For example, governments often seek public support before they enter wars. And governments sometimes gain this support by having their views mirrored in the media. Critics argue that this is an example of the media failing to provide a check on the government. Instead of curbing government power, the media enables it.

Media bias often decreases when a war lasts for a long period of time. As the war continues, news about deaths tends to gain more attention. This news can begin to show the conflict's costs. Over time, politicians also develop a wider range of opinions. In response, news outlets report more viewpoints about the conflict. Then people gain access to more opinions and information. Those changes can cause shifts in public opinion.

▲ In 1968, public opinion turned against the Vietnam War when news media began discussing the heavy death tolls.

At home and abroad, politics has enormous impacts. News media are primary ways people learn about politics. The media also affects how citizens participate in politics. At its best, politics reporting can make people informed and engaged. When that happens, democracy can become stronger.

FOCUS ON
BIAS IN REPORTING ON POLITICS

Write your answers on a separate piece of paper.

1. Write a paragraph explaining the main ideas of Chapter 4.

2. Do you think news media should avoid favoring one political party? Why or why not?

3. According to politics experts, what kind of reporting can lower people's trust in politics?

> **A.** coverage of local politics
> **B.** horse-race coverage
> **C.** detailed coverage of policies

4. Why might getting less media attention hurt a candidate's chance of being elected?

> **A.** Media attention tends to focus only on a candidate's policy stances.
> **B.** People rarely learn about a candidate from news media.
> **C.** People are less likely to vote for a candidate they know little about.

Answer key on page 48.

GLOSSARY

algorithms
Steps that a computer must follow to complete a process.

bias
An attitude that causes someone to treat certain ideas unfairly.

climate change
A human-caused global crisis involving long-term changes in Earth's temperature and weather patterns.

context
Related information that can make something easier to understand.

controversial
Likely to be argued about.

election fraud
The crime of interfering with an election, either by adding or taking away votes, to change the election's result.

frame
To discuss a topic in a certain way.

objective
Showing facts rather than opinions.

partisan
Biased in favor of a particular group, usually a political group.

policy
A plan or strategy for addressing a specific issue, often through government action.

transparency
Openness and honesty in sharing information.

TO LEARN MORE

BOOKS

Fleischer, Jeff. *Votes of Confidence: A Young Person's Guide to American Elections*, 2nd Ed. Minneapolis: Lerner Publications, 2020.

Harris, Duchess, with Laura K. Murray. *Uncovering Bias in the News*. Minneapolis: Abdo Publishing, 2018.

Mara, Wil. *Politics and the Media*. Ann Arbor, MI: Cherry Lake Publishing, 2019.

NOTE TO EDUCATORS

Visit **www.focusreaders.com** to find lesson plans, activities, links, and other resources related to this title.

INDEX

Answer Key: 1. Answers will vary; 2. Answers will vary; 3. B; 4. C